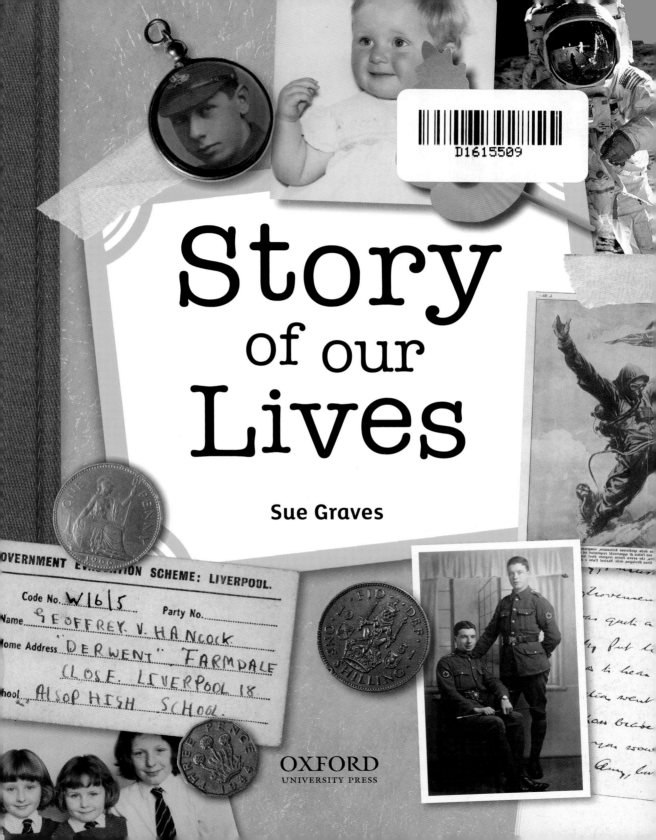

Story
of our
Lives

Sue Graves

OVERNMENT EVACUATION SCHEME: LIVERPOOL.

Code No. W16/5.   Party No.

Name GEOFFREY. V. HANCOCK.

Home Address "DERWENT" FARMDALE

CLOSE. LIVERPOOL 18.

School ALSOP HIGH SCHOOL.

OXFORD
UNIVERSITY PRESS

Contents

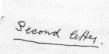

The Hancock Family

This is the Hancock family and this is their family album.

It's a scrapbook of photos, letters and objects that remind them of important events in their lives. It also includes many world events that they have seen.

Hancock Family Tree

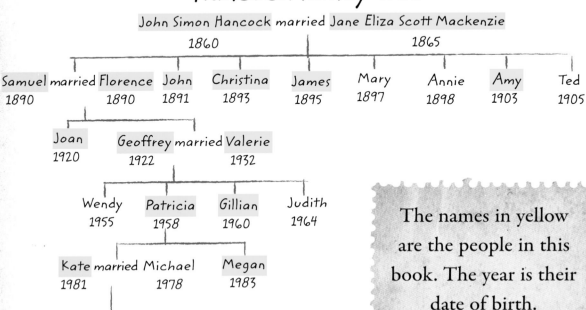

John Simon Hancock married Jane Eliza Scott Mackenzie
1860 — 1865

Samuel married Florence	John	Christina	James	Mary	Annie	Amy	Ted
1890 — 1890	1891	1893	1895	1897	1898	1903	1905

Joan 1920 — Geoffrey married Valerie
1922 — 1932

Wendy	Patricia	Gillian	Judith
1955	1958	1960	1964

Kate married Michael — Megan
1981 — 1978 — 1983

Leo
2012

The names in yellow are the people in this book. The year is their date of birth.

Queen Victoria

Queen Victoria's Diamond **Jubilee** was in 1897. She had been queen for 60 years.

Queen Victoria

During Queen Victoria's **reign**, John Hancock and his wife, Jane, lived in Liverpool. They had eight children! Here are four of them.

Samuel, James, John and Christina

A special display

John and Jane's eldest son, Samuel, watched a special display of ships on the River Mersey in Liverpool. They were part of the jubilee celebrations. The ships were decorated with flags and **bunting**.

1897   2014

World War I

World War I began after Archduke Franz Ferdinand of Austria was shot dead. The war lasted from 1914 until 1918. Millions of people were killed or injured.

A brave soldier

Samuel Hancock fought in World War I. He joined the army with two of his brothers, James and John. Sadly, only Samuel returned from the war. His brothers, John and James, were both killed.

Archduke
Franz Ferdinand

Samuel and James
Hancock in uniform

1897

1914–1918

2014

A special letter

John trained to be a soldier at an army camp in Blackpool. He wrote this letter to his little sister Amy before he left for France. In it he tells her not to worry about him. The letter was written two months before he died.

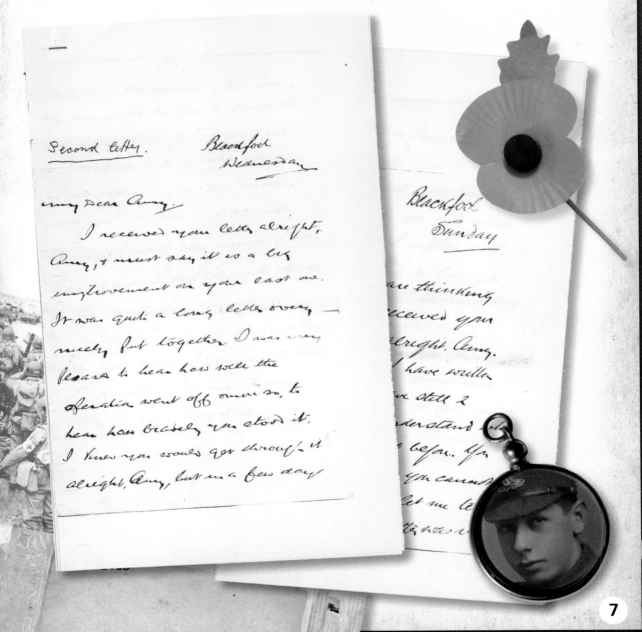

Tutankhamun's Tomb

After the war, Samuel married Florence. They had two children, Joan and Geoffrey. Geoffrey was born in 1922.

The week after Geoffrey was born, Tutankhamun's **tomb** was discovered in Egypt.

La luce finalmente nelle tenebre trimillenarie di Tutankamen.

Tutankhamun was a **pharaoh** of Ancient Egypt. His tomb was found by two British **archaeologists**. They were called Lord Carnarvon and Howard Carter.

The opening of the tomb in 1922

A pharaoh's curse

Some people believed the pharaoh's tomb was **cursed**.
They said that anyone who opened it would die soon after.
No one knows if this is true, but Lord Carnarvon died just
a few weeks later.

Some of the tomb's treasures

World War II

World War II began when Germany invaded Poland in 1939. The war spread to many countries around the world, including the UK.

Germany invades Poland. The war begins ...

on land

at sea

in the air

Victory at last!

Evacuation

Geoffrey Hancock, like many children, was **evacuated** to the countryside. He was sent to Wales. He had to wear this evacuation ticket when he travelled.

GOVERNMENT EVACUATION SCHEME: LIVERPOOL

Code No. W1615
Party No.
Name GEOFFREY V. HANCOCK
Home Address "DERWENT" FARMDALE
CLOSE. LIVERPOOL 18
School ALSOP HIGH SCHOOL.

Geoffrey Hancock in his air force uniform

Joining up

On his 18th birthday Geoffrey joined the Royal Air Force. He became a rear gunner. It was his job to sit at the back of a plane and fire a machine gun at enemy planes. Geoffrey was later injured during a **bombing raid**.

1897   1939–1945   2014

Mount Everest

The **coronation** of Queen Elizabeth II took place in Westminster Abbey on 2nd June, 1953. Geoffrey met his wife, Valerie, just before this.

The coronation

Geoffrey and Valerie on their wedding day

1953 was an important year for them – and for the rest of the world, too!

On the same day as the Queen's coronation there was even more exciting news. Edmund Hillary and Sherpa Tenzing Norgay had climbed to the top of Mount Everest. They were the first people known to have done this.

Mount Everest

News reports

Geoffrey and Valerie read about the **conquest** of Mount Everest in the newspapers. They heard about it on the radio, too.

Edmund Hillary and Sherpa Tenzing Norgay

Conquistata la vetta del mondo. Una cordata della spedizione britannica, composta dal dalla guida nepalese Tensing, ha raggiunto, con l'aiuto di apparecchi respiratori ad ossige (m. 8888) la massima elevazione della Terra, che aveva finora respinto dieci tentativi. spiegate al vento tre piccole bandiere: della Gran Bretagna, delle Nazioni Unite e del Ne

1897   1953   2014

Munich Air Crash

Geoffrey Hancock was a fan of Manchester United Football Club. In February 1958, he heard some sad news. The football team were in a plane crash at Munich airport in Germany. The crash happened in very bad weather. It killed a lot of people, including some of the players.

The Manchester United football team

The Munich air crash

The investigation

Different **investigators** tried to find out why the plane had crashed. A British team discovered that **slush** on the runway had caused the accident.

THE ILLUSTRATED LONDON NEWS

SATURDAY, FEBRUARY 15, 1958.

THE AIR DISASTER AT MUNICH: BURNING WRECKAGE OF THE *ELIZABETHAN* AFTER THE CRASH IN WHICH TWENTY-ONE LOST THEIR LIVES, INCLUDING SEVEN MEMBERS OF THE MANCHESTER UNITED FOOTBALL TEAM.

Patricia

Geoffrey and Valerie's daughter, Patricia, was born in 1958. Geoffrey read the newspaper reports about the crash to Valerie as she looked after baby Patricia.

1897   1958   2014

Moon Landings

In 1969, an American **astronaut** called Neil Armstrong became the first person to walk on the Moon. He spent two and a half hours on the Moon's surface.

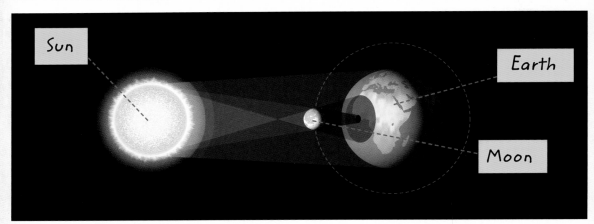

Sun

Earth

Moon

Between 1969 and 1972, 12 men landed on the Moon. They found out a lot about it!

Neil Armstrong on the Moon's surface

Moon rock sample

Moon buggy

Gill and Patricia

A school project

Patricia and her sister, Gill, were at the same school and did a project on the Moon landings. Patricia was 11 years old and Gill was 9. Patricia, Gill and their friends watched Neil Armstrong landing on the Moon on their TV at home. It was very exciting!

1897

1969

2014

Nelson Mandela

In 1963, a man named Nelson Mandela was sent to prison in South Africa. He disagreed with the **government** of his country, which said that black and white people had to live apart. Nelson Mandela believed this was wrong. He spent 27 years in prison for trying to change this system.

Nelson Mandela, 1918–2013

People all over the world **protested** about Mandela's imprisonment.

On 11th February 1990 he was set free.

Nelson and his wife, Winnie Mandela

A special assembly

Patricia's daughters, Kate and Megan, were in primary school when Nelson Mandela was released from prison. They remember learning about him in a special school assembly.

Kate and Megan

1897   1990   2014

Barack Obama

On 20th January 2009, Barack Obama became the first African-American president of the United States of America.

Barack Obama makes history

Patricia was the headteacher of a school when Barack was elected. She held a special assembly at her school.

1897   2009   2014

A special celebration

In 2014, Geoffrey and Valerie Hancock had been married for 60 years. They had a big party for all their family and friends to celebrate. Best of all, the Queen sent a card to congratulate them.

The Hancock family are looking forward to celebrating many more family and world events.

I am so pleased to know that you are celebrating your Diamond Wedding anniversary on 3rd April, 2014. I send my congratulations and best wishes to you on such a special occasion.

Elizabeth R

Mr. and Mrs. Geoffrey Hancock

Take a look in your own family album and see what you can find!

Glossary

archaeologists: people who study ancient society

astronaut: person trained to fly and travel in a spacecraft

bombing raid: attack on a city by planes dropping bombs

bunting: line of small flags on a string used for decoration

conquest: a victory over something

coronation: crowning of a king or queen

cursed: affected by very bad luck

evacuated: sent away from the city to the countryside for safety

government: group of people who are in charge of a country

investigators: people who find out facts about something

jubilee: special anniversary

pharaoh: ruler in Ancient Egypt

protested: complained about something believed to be wrong

reign: period of time when a king or queen rules

slush: snow that is beginning to melt

tomb: place where a dead body is buried

Index

About the Author

I'm a children's author and write fiction, non-fiction, poetry and plays. I love sport and I play tennis, badminton and golf. In my spare time I paint watercolours and enjoy both visiting and taking part in exhibitions. I'm married and have four children and seven grandchildren.

Greg Foot, Series Editor

I've loved science ever since the day I took my papier mâché volcano into school. I filled it with far too much baking powder, vinegar and red food colouring, and WHOOSH! I covered the classroom ceiling in red goo. Now I've got the best job in the world: I present TV shows for the BBC, answer kids' science questions on YouTube, and make huge explosions on stage at festivals!

Working on TreeTops inFact has been great fun. There are so many brilliant books, and guess what ... they're all packed full of awesome facts! What's your favourite?